D0832665

FROM MRS MORRISON.

TO TERR/

CHRISTMAS 1960

This, children, is a new book about British birds and their nests. All the birds are common ones, and Allen Seaby has given you lovely coloured pictures, to enable you to recognise each of the birds when you see them.

I have tried to tell you a little about each bird, so that you will know where and how they live; but the great thing is to know what the bird is when you see it, and you can only do that by watching and keeping your eyes open. So you want to look at these lovely pictures very closely, and then go out and see how many of the birds in this book you can find. You can try to find their nests as well, but if you do, do not take the eggs—just look at them.

Good Hunting!

Brian Vesey-Fitzgerald.

Series 536

BRITISH BIRDS

AND THEIR NESTS

By

BRIAN VESEY-FITZGERALD, F.L.S.

Colour Illustrations by

ALLEN W. SEABY

Publishers: Wills & Hepworth Ltd., Loughborough

Printed in England

The Yellowhammer

This is the little tubby bird, with the bright yellow cap, that sits on the telegraph wires or the very tops of the hedges, and sings to you as you pass by; "*A-little-bit-of-bread-and-no-cheee-ee-se*".

The Yellowhammer builds a very neat and tidy nest close to the ground (sometimes right on it), in a bush or on a hedgebank.

This bird does a great deal of good, for the Yellowhammer eats hardly anything but insects, and catches many more to feed its chicks. It seems to sing all day long, too, and is a very busy, happy little bird.

The Wren

The Wren is our smallest common bird. It is only three-and-a-half inches long and weighs only one-third of an ounce, which is about the same weight as an ordinary envelope and a sheet of notepaper.

Wrens like to live in gardens near houses (as well as in the country), and run up and down the tree trunks, banks and walls, looking like little mice, and stopping every now and then to sing their cheerful, shrill little songs.

The Wren builds a beautiful little nest, shaped like a ball, with a hole at the side. It is always close to the ground and usually very well hidden.

The Robin

Everybody knows the Robin Redbreast. Robins are so tame that they will come and sit on your spade while you are gardening, and it is quite easy to get them to eat from your hand. They eat a lot of worms and small snails, and are very good friends to gardeners.

Robins often build their nests in garden sheds, but they also like to build them in old boots, tin cans and so on. You cannot tell the difference between the cock and hen birds, for both are redbreasted exactly alike. Though so friendly to us, Robins are very quarrelsome amongst themselves and spend a lot of time fighting each other.

The Blue Tit

This lovely little bird is very common in gardens and towns, and will eat almost anything. If you put out food on a bird table in your garden, the Blue Tits will come for it and soon get very tame; or when you hang up a lump of fat or a coconut, they will cling to it upside down to eat, and look very pretty

If you put up a nest box, the Blue Tits are almost certain to come and nest in your garden. They are also very fond of pecking off the caps of milk-bottles when left on the doorstep in the morning.

The Long-tailed Tit

The Long-tailed Tit likes places where there are gorse and thorn bushes. It is a very small bird, but looks bigger than it is, because its tail is longer than its body.

The nest is the most marvellous of all the nests of British birds. It is shaped like a bottle, and made of moss and wool, hair and cobwebs, and is lined with hundreds and hundreds of feathers. The bird gets into the nest, and shapes it by turning round and round, pressing the feathers flat with its breast, like the bird in the picture is doing. Then a roof is put on, and a tiny doorway made in the side.

The Bullfinch

The Bullfinch is one of our most beautiful birds, but it is not very common and, being most shy, is only seldom seen.

Bullfinches will sometimes live in large gardens, but they like the edges of woods and thick hedges and thorn bushes. They are fond of fruit buds and blossom, and often Bullfinches will come into gardens when the fruit blossom is out in the spring, sit up in the trees and pull it off, so gardeners do not like to see these birds about the place.

The nest is made of twigs, lined with hair, and is just a shallow cup, not easy to see.

The Linnet

The Linnet is another very common bird. In the summer, Linnets prefer to live on commons with gorse bushes, or down by the seashore where there are sandhills; but in the winter, they gather together into big flocks and visit farm land and farmyards.

Linnets have a very sweet low song, but when they call to each other the sound is rather like someone playing a banjo.

The cock Linnet has a lovely crimson breast, as you see in the picture, while the hen is just a small brown bird.

The nest is often in a gorse bush and is built quite close to the ground, but not on it.

The Jay

The Jay, as you can see, is a very beautiful bird.

Jays live in woods as a rule, but a few come into parks and gardens in towns. Their voices are not nearly so beautiful as their feathers—being just a loud scream—and as soon as you go into a wood where Jays live, they screech at you, warning all the other birds that you are coming.

In fact, Jays are not nearly so nice as they look, for they steal other birds' eggs, and sometimes kill and eat little birds as well.

Jays are also very fond of green peas.

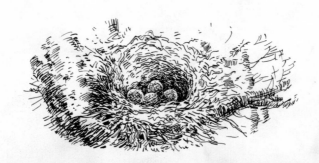

The Starling

Starlings are very common. In the winter they come to towns in thousands to sleep at night, and go out into the country again in the daytime. Those that live far away from a town will gather together in great crowds at night in the woods or reed beds by the sides of ponds.

The Starlings nest in towns, too, and are very fond of building in chimney pots (often causing fires to puff the smoke into our rooms because the birds' nests prevent it escaping the proper way), and they also like to build in drainpipes round the roof.

Starlings are very clever at imitating the songs of other birds.

The Magpie

The Magpie, like the Jay, is a very beautiful bird with a rather nasty nature. It is, in fact, a cousin of the Jay.

Magpies build wonderful nests high up in trees. They are very big and strong, and when finished the birds put roofs of thorny sticks on top, turning their homes into fortresses. They like big gardens just outside towns as well as thick hedges in the country, and are such big birds that you cannot help seeing them.

Magpies kill young birds and steal eggs, but they do much less harm in gardens than Jays.

The Blackbird

The Blackbird is the very black bird with a bright yellow beak that you see in the garden, and is one of the commonest birds in England. It is only the cock that is black with a yellow beak, for the hen is a dark brown bird.

The Blackbird has one of the loveliest of all bird songs, and if you look closely you will see that it likes to sing from the same place at about the same time each day.

It is very fond of fruit and steals a lot of our currants, raspberries and strawberries; but it also eats many insects.

The Song Thrush

Like the Blackbird, the Song Thrush is a common bird in towns and gardens. It has a lovely song, too, but while the Blackbird does not sing for very long in the year, the Song Thrush sings in almost every month. It likes to get on to a high post or tall tree to sing in the evening.

Song Thrushes are very fond of snails to eat. They catch the snails and then take them to a big stone and hammer them on it until the shells break.

You can always tell a Thrush's nest from that of a Blackbird, because the Thrush does not line its nest like the Blackbird.

The Goldfinch

This brilliantly coloured little bird likes to live in gardens and orchards. The cock and hen are just the same, so that you cannot tell which is which. (In the picture there is a full grown Goldfinch and a young one).

The beautiful little nest is almost always built near houses, and is usually put near the end of a thin branch at a good height.

Though Goldfinches live so much in gardens, they do not do much harm, for they eat a lot of insects as well as seeds. In the winter, Goldfinches leave the villages and gardens to go out into the fields and woods.

The Willow Warbler

Some people call this bird the Willow Wren. It is a very small bird, which comes to England every spring from North Africa over the Mediterranean, going back again in September. It generally gets here about the end of March, and in the summer is one of the commonest birds in the country.

The nest is shaped like a ball and is placed on the ground, but the hole in the side is much bigger than in a Wren's nest.

You do not often see the Willow Warbler, because it likes to get into the middle of a tree and is very much the same colour as the leaves.

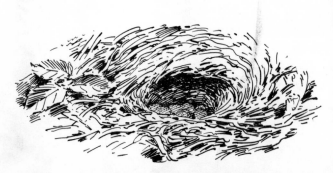

The House Martin

The House Martin also comes to us in the spring from Africa, and usually arrives about the middle of April.

It likes to build its nest on the wall of a house or barn, just underneath the eaves. The nest is made of mud or clay and is lined with straw and feathers. Very often the House Martin returns to its old nest and repairs it for use again.

You can always tell House Martins from Swallows, because of the white patch above their tails as they fly away from you (like the one in the picture). Swallows have not got a white patch.

The Turtle Dove

The Turtle Dove is another bird that comes to us in early summer from Africa over the Mediterranean, but it usually stays in the south or east of England, and only rarely in the north. It arrives in May and leaves again in September.

The Turtle Dove makes a lovely, lazy purr like a cat, but with a double note: "*Purr-purr*!" It is very similar to the Pigeon, as you can see from the picture, and likes company, so there are usually several Turtle Doves' nests together.

Turtle Doves eat grain, seeds and berries, but not insects.

The Green Woodpecker

Country people often call the Green Woodpecker the " yaffle," because of its call, which is like a laugh. It is a fine, big bird, and often comes on to garden lawns to dig for ants.

The nest is in the hole of a tree, which the bird makes for itself by hammering it out with its very sharp beak.

When the Green Woodpecker flies away from you, the bright yellow patch above its tail can be seen (as you see it in the picture) and then it looks a yellow bird. The flight is dipping—up and down—as if it cannot fly very well or is too heavy.

The Pied Wagtail

Lots of people call this bird the Water Wagtail, because it does like to be fairly near water. The bird in the picture is a hen, but the cock Pied Wagtail has a black back. It is a common bird, and likes to live near buildings.

The Pied Wagtail is very fond of following the plough on a farm, and of being near cows in a field, so that it can catch the insects which these big things disturb. The Wagtail likes walking about on lawns, flicking its tail as it walks, and cleverly jumping up and catching insects as they fly past. Country people sometimes call this bird the "dishwasher".

The Kingfisher

You must go to the rivers or lakes, canals or big ponds, if you want to see this gorgeously coloured bird.

The Kingfisher lives almost entirely on fish, which it catches by diving into the water, seizing the fish in its beak by the middle as it swims by. The bird then throws the fish into the air and catches it again to swallow it head first.

The nest is usually at the end of a tunnel, about three feet long, made in a hole in a bank. The Kingfisher makes the tunnel itself and then lines its nest with fishbones, which smell dreadfully.

The Brown Owl

The Brown Owl is often called the Tawny Owl. This is the bird that calls "*tu-whit, tu-whoo*," at night. It is a large bird, almost as big as a Rook, and it nests in hollow trees. In the daytime, the Brown Owl sits close up to the trunk of a tree (just as you see in the picture) and sleeps most of the time.

Brown Owls are quite common, and often live right in the middle of big towns. They are also very great friends of man, for Owls eat mice, voles and rats, which are all animals that do a lot of damage to our food supplies.

The Moorhen

The Moorhen is an extremely common bird on ponds and lakes, and even on big ditches. You must have seen it, for this bird is equally at home on ponds in town parks.

Moorhens swim in jerks, as though someone was pulling them along with a bit of string, their heads bobbing up and down and also their white tails. The chicks can swim almost as soon as they are hatched, and they are so light that they can walk about on leaves floating on the water.

Moorhens eat water plants and insects, and are fond of worms.

The Black-headed Gull

This is the commonest Gull in England, which you see far inland following the plough on farms, or flying up and down rivers. This is also the Gull that flies along the Thames Embankment in London, waiting for people to throw it food.

The head is not really black, as you can see, and in the winter it is quite white, but you can always tell the Black-headed Gull by the crimson colour of its legs. This bird nests in huge colonies and the nests are on the ground.

These Gulls are becoming more and more land birds, while some of them never go to the seashore at all.